BULLYING

Anti Bullying Guide For All Ages

Dr. Nelly

HOW TO STOP THE BULLYING

Anti bullying guide for all ages

By Dr. Nelly a lecturer, medical & health practitioner.

Table of contents

INTRODUCTION

Harassing or bullying can most effectively be characterized as a system in which force, misuse, danger, or pressure is utilized to scare or rule another party forcefully. There can be numerous different thought processes which menaces could have for tormenting some other person.

This kind of conduct is ongoing and rehashed in most of the cases. There is likewise an essential for harassing. Also, as per different specialists and different specialists, that essential is the basic impression of unevenness. This irregularity can be concerning actual design, actual power, or social power. There are likewise numerous specialists who hold the assessment that tormenting is a complicated strategy and hence, there can be no basic definition for harassing. Harassing can have many adverse results and impacts. Also, thus, there have been many discussions on the subject of in the event that harassers ought to be shipped off remedial offices or prisons.

Prologue to bullying

Bullying is an idea which is somewhat difficult to comprehend. Hence, characterizing tormenting in careful or substantial terms is very troublesome. Notwithstanding, it tends to be said with conviction that harassing is a sort of forceful way of behaving which is performed with the principal point of hurting the other party. There can be various justifications for why an individual may be tormenting another person. As indicated by different authority reports, tormenting could happen among kids as youthful as four-year-old. Consequently, all guardians must ensure that they can show youngsters what comprises tormenting and why it ought not be finished no matter what.

There have been a ton of studies which were finished on this specific theme. Furthermore, a large portion of those reviews appear to concur that all harassing standards of conduct have three principal qualities. Also, those three principal attributes are:

An unfriendly goal
A reasonable irregularity in power between the gatherings in question
The hurtful standard of conduct happening as a propensity or throughout some stretch of time
Aside from these three fundamental qualities, perusers must recall that harassing can have pessimistic physical, mental, and close to home ramifications for every one of the gatherings associated with the long run. Consequently, it is critical to recognize such standards of conduct and end those personal conduct standards straightaway.

The Impacts of bullying

It has been laid out by different examinations and reports that harassing is unsafe and it can adversely affect the physical, social, close to home, and mental self of the relative multitude of gatherings included. There are a few situations wherein the force of harassing is expanded so much that the individual frequently winds up ending it all. There are additionally numerous other adverse consequences of tormenting. Furthermore, a portion of those impacts are:

Persistent Discouragement

Melancholy is a temperament problem which is by and large portrayed by a singular inclination desolate, miserable, or losing interest in exercises which were viewed as pleasurable for a lengthy timeframe. This is a significant mental problem which can have pessimistic ramifications for the individual languishing as well as over those present in their general climate. As indicated by different investigations, the gamble of sadness increments on the off chance that an individual has experienced tormenting.

Expanded Pace of Self destruction Contemplations, Plans, and Endeavors

It has been tracked down by the World Wellbeing Association (WHO) that harassing can expand the general gamble of self destruction plans, contemplations, and endeavors for the casualty dramatically.

Nervousness Confusion

This is one more mental problem which has been firmly connected to harassing. Numerous casualties of tormenting experience the ill effects of a nervousness problem.
Aside from the impacts, there can be numerous other adverse consequences of harassing for both the person in question and the harasser like unfortunate general wellbeing and enjoying pointless standards of conduct.

Should Menaces be shipped off Remedial Offices?

As per the Middle for Infectious prevention (CDC), just about 4,400 passings happen because of self destruction caused as a result of harassing every year in the US of America along. This number gets fundamentally high in nations like India, which is positioned third most elevated as far as fruitful self destruction endeavors with the excellent justification behind tormenting. This demonstrates how very essential it is to take a legitimate position against all domineering jerks regardless of the age. Nonetheless, that position should be painstakingly built and thoroughly considered. Tormenting can happen at all ages and can be run in its seriousness. What may be viewed as tormenting for one could be thought of as laid back diversion for another person. Thus, it is vital to set some fundamental guidelines concerning what is OK and what isn't.

There can be situations in which one can essentially be guided in regards to improper way of behaving which may be destructive to others. For individuals who show rehashed personal conduct standards of harassing even of little power, it is significant those individuals be shipped off restorative offices. Likewise, on the off chance that there is a harasser who has no respect for others and has shown a very forceful personal conduct standard of tormenting even once then the individual ought to be shipped off a remedial office of some kind or another. There are various justifications for why this ought to be finished and a portion of those reasons are referenced underneath.

Need Proficient Assistance

There have been many investigations which show that harassers frequently experience the ill effects of some kind of physical, profound, or mental injury. Signing up for a rectification office can assist menaces with managing those issues and get once again to life more grounded than any time in recent memory.

Equity for the People in question

Menaces frequently put the casualties through a ton of harsh results. This frequently winds up having various destructive impacts on the existence of the person in question and thus, it is normal for the casualty to want for that domineering jerk to disappear. Shipping off the harasser to a restorative office will give the casualty space which would be important for the casualty to think about the whole injury.

A Way to Recuperation

A few harassers don't understand the full degree of the activities. Menaces frequently experience the ill effects of injury themselves. Furthermore, that is the reason going to a restorative office can be helpful for both the gatherings in question.

The Gamble of Self destruction

With regards to harassing, then there is a significant gamble of self destruction included. Subsequently, it is significant for a grown-up or the power figure to guarantee that the gamble of self destruction is all around as limited as could really be expected. One incredible method for accomplishing that is by sending the domineering jerk away to a remedial office.

CHAPTER 1

THE PSYCHOLOGY OF BULLYING

Many individuals experience tormenting sooner or later in their lives. Regardless of whether they aren't its immediate objective, they might observer it at school, in the work environment, or even at home. Anybody can turn into a harasser, and the purposes behind tormenting change generally. Understanding the brain science of harassing culprits can assist you with getting a handle on why somebody could decide to menace. There is no defense for tormenting. Nonetheless, understanding this unsafe way of behaving may assist somebody with adapting to it more actually, understanding that it has considerably more to do with the harasser's own irritating private matters than whatever they could have done to cause it.

In the public eye, there are different elements that drive menaces. Regardless of the poisonousness of this way of behaving, understanding its brain science is critical to taking further steps against harassing. Individuals normally become menaces for an explanation, paying little mind to how horrible their way of behaving may be. The following are a portion of the potential underlying drivers.

Seen Dangers

By and large, when menaces home in on somebody, they see this individual as a danger. The objective of harassing might be "unique" or generally extraordinary such that stands apart to the domineering jerk. Menaces frequently single out people whom they view as a danger, whether this is a danger to their potential business achievement, inner self, or confidence. Whether somebody really represents some sort of danger by being "unique" canvary. In any case, the activities of menaces are not legitimized. Generally speaking, harassers are just subliminally mindful that they're feeling compromised by another person.

Desire For Power

We experience a daily reality such that an accentuation is put on power and getting however much of it as could reasonably be expected. Tragically, there are numerous people who assimilate this and trust that thumping others down is the best method for developing themselves. This is particularly normal when individuals are designated in the working environment or in different groups of friends. Some of the time, this returns to menaces feeling compromised by the people whom they focus with their terrible way of behaving. In different cases, menaces wish to impart dread in others as a way to acquire power; they couldn't care less about the objective of their way of behaving being a loss from their journey for power and control.

Retribution

One of the less generally examined inspirations of menaces is retribution. There are sure times when menaces really accept that their objective violated them (or somebody they care about) at some point. Whether this conviction is exact relies upon the exact idea of the conditions; be that as it may, tormenting is never the response. On the off chance that somebody did as a matter of fact foul up, it depends on the individual violated to fittingly report the make a difference to the legitimate power figures or defy the individual, as opposed to turn into a harasser themselves. Vigilante equity and vengeance missions have an interminable penchant to turn out badly and can exacerbate the situation for all interested parties.

At times, menaces target blameless others on the grounds that the harasser was hurt by somebody previously. This could be persuaded by retribution or an endeavor to reclaim the power that was once taken from them previously. Once more, this doesn't pardon the way of behaving of harming another person yet is just an endeavor to comprehend where this conduct could emerge out of.

Weakness

The web-based world and virtual entertainment have numerous potential gains, yet they've additionally made the way for cyberbullying. In that capacity, there's turned into another peculiarity of individuals taking cover behind fake records to target another person on the web. Some of the time, these harassers actually know their objectives. Now and again they don't. Numerous cyberbullies have private matters occurring in their lives, thus their craving to target others as they cover their own characters. Not all cyberbullies are covered up; there are sure culprits of online disdain who have no issue utilizing their name and picture, yet numerous cyberbullies in all actuality do take cover behind their screens and phony web-based entertainment accounts.

It is frequently more straightforward to go after somebody when they are not in your nearby presence, and numerous cyberbullies get sensations of joy when others "like" or focus on their assaults on others.

Perversion

Unadulterated perversion is unquestionably a component with specific harassers and demonstrates a more obsessive or even sociopathic drive behind their activities. Certain individuals who simply appreciate are having the option to put down others. We see this in harmful connections and in lawbreakers who proceed to target people who fit a specific form. At the point when twistedness is the most grounded factor behind a harasser's activities, they are likelier to be considerably more perilous than menaces driven by different variables since they don't have an inner voice or sensations of regret.

Menaces And Unsettled Past Injury

From the outset, culprits might appear to be strong, predominant, and in charge. After nearer assessment, there are many cases in which menaces have unsettled injury from their pasts. At the point when private matters aren't managed in the proper way, they don't disappear, paying little heed to what lengths individuals will go for them to. Generally speaking, they lay on pause, underneath the surface, deteriorating and more terrible. At last, unsettled injury can at this point not be held back and starts to appear in appalling ways. Tormenting others is one of numerous awful manners by which unsettled injury can show.

Tragically, there are times when previous overcomers of harassing proceed to become menaces themselves. They might in any case be battling with what has been going on with them previously. In different cases, these individuals might accept that harassing others is the best way to protect themselves from present-day menaces actually. This defective perspective frequently just proceeds with the poisonous, endless loop of harassing. The effects of harassing are very proven and factual; proceeding to turn into a domineering jerk oneself is one more effect on know about.

The Significance Of Halting Domineering jerks

Understanding the mental factors and urges behind domineering jerks is foremost to halting them. By and large, the onus is put on the objectives of menaces. These individuals are frequently told to report the episode or in any case make a move to keep themselves from being additionally designated. Nonetheless, putting the onus on the culprits of harmful way of behaving is basic, as it considers them responsible for their way of behaving.

Not Remunerating Awful Way of behaving

The ascent of against harassing efforts and stages might make the deception that domineering jerks are never compensated for their terrible way of behaving. Tragically, this basically isn't correct. There are many cases in which menaces are seen as more remarkable and predominant while they're putting others down.

Deliberately ignoring the activities of menaces in a roundabout way remunerates the way of behaving.

Anything which doesn't quit tormenting innately compensates it, paying little heed to how unobtrusive it very well might be. Here and there, individuals overlook menaces since they would rather not be tormented, however this attitude is dangerous. It shows indifference with regards to the people who are as of now being focused on and doesn't ensure that harassers won't turn on others one day.

Genuine strength and power don't depend after putting others down. Somebody who is areas of strength for genuinely strong can sparkle and lift without tormenting others.

The Advancement Of Emotional well-being And Health

Understanding the mental variables behind a domineering jerk's terrible way of behaving is unquestionably significant. Be that as it may, advancing psychological well-being and health is one more extraordinary approach to stopping harassing. This can help survivors, spectators, menaces, and potential domineering jerks the same. Individuals who have seen or been exposed to harassing need to mend similarly however much people who incur agony and mischief upon others.

Harassing isn't solid. Regardless of how rich, fruitful, famous, or generally well-off a harasser might give off an impression of being, the purposeful abuse of others connotes a problem.Likewise, being designated by a domineering jerk doesn't imply that somebody is frail. Regardless of the ascent of consideration that harassing has gotten throughout the course of recent years, there are as yet specific connotations that recommend just powerless individuals are tormented. Indeed, this sort of outlook finds fault with people who are designated, instead of those doing the tormenting.

CHAPTER 2

WARNING SIGNALS OF BULLYING

Nobody ought to need to tolerate harassing. It can cause individuals to feel perilous at school and hopeless when they return home.

The accompanying will furnish you with the abilities to detect various indications of harassing and a portion of the side effects that could emerge out of this.

Close to home and conduct indications of harassing

Changes in rest designs
Changes in eating designs
Regular tears or outrage
Temperament swings
Feels sick in the first part of the day
Becomes removed or begins stammering
Becomes forceful and irrational
Won't discuss what's up
Starts to target kin
Consistently 'loses' cash or starts taking.

Actual indications of tormenting

Has unexplained injuries, cuts, scratches

Returns home with absent or harmed effects or garments

Returns home hungry.

School indications of tormenting

Doesn't have any desire to go to class

Changes their course to the everyday schedule scared of strolling to school

Doesn't have any desire to go to class on the transport/cable car/train

School grades start to fall.

Different indications of harassing

Here and there indications of tormenting can be undeniably more covered up. They can include:

Frequently alone or prohibited from kinship bunches at school

An incessant objective for prodding, copying or scorn at school

Unfit to shout out in class and seems uncertain or scared.

CHAPTER 3

THE SOCIOPATHS AND PSYCHOPATHS

A few instances of positive administration of difficulties can begin surfacing when we see some hidden inadvertent reasoning for an event of activities towards us. Take for a moment

a maniac who pours water all around your lovely dress or Shirt, your response however not all that sweet yet you will basically think about put such a situation behind and proceed with your day action essentially on the grounds that you know and comprehend the culprit is a crazy person. Anything that you do to communicate your resentment might have practically no impact on the grounds that the distraught individual won't ever grasp your response. The possibility of "so grieved, such a crazy person " jumps into your head and you may over the long haul feel terrible for such a horrendous condition. This really leaves you with no miserable inclination about your lovely dress or Shirt.

Who are sociopaths?

The term sociopath alludes to somebody living with total disregard for other people (ASPD) — as does the term insane person.

The latest release of the "Demonstrative and Factual Manual of Mental Issues" (DSM-5), which emotional well-being experts use to analyze emotional wellness conditions, characterizes ASPD as a reliable dismissal for rules and normal practices and rehashed infringement of others' privileges.

Individuals with the condition could appear to be enchanting and appealling from the get go, by all accounts, however they by and large find it hard to figure out others' sentiments. They frequently:

defy guidelines or regulations
act forcefully or imprudently
feel little culpability for hurt they cause others
use control, misleading, and controlling way of behaving.

LANGUAGE MATTERS
Both sociopathy and psychopathy have become all around perceived terms among emotional well-being experts, yet neither address an authority conclusion. They likewise convey a ton of shame, especially for individuals living with behavioral conditions, so it's ideal

to abstain from portraying anybody showing vicious or manipulative way of behaving as "sociopaths" or "insane people."

All things considered, center around unambiguous ways of behaving and activities. Instead of marking a controlling ex as a sociopath, for instance, you could say, "He would routinely remind me he was checking my web-based entertainment action."

Specialists initially started utilizing the term sociopath during the 1930sTrusted Source. In contrast to "psychopathy," it wasn't effortlessly mistaken for "psychosis." The prefix likewise mirrored a generally held conviction that the qualities and ways of behaving related with sociopathy connected with socio-natural elements.

Numerous scientists utilized sociopathy and psychopathy conversely until ASPD was added to the third release of the DSM in 1980.

What's the contrast between a sociopath and a mental case?
In a clinical setting, there's no real distinction among sociopathy and psychopathy. An emotional well-being proficient will not analyze both of the two.

A few therapists and scientists truly do make key differentiations among sociopathy and psychopathy.

However, these terms basically offer two marginally various approaches to grasping the conclusion of ASPD

In these understandings, psychopathy is here and there seen as including more arranged conduct. The way of behaving could not really be brutal, yet all at once it's commonly planned.

Research upholds a couple of these qualifications — to a degree.

Robert Bunny, the clinician who made the Psychopathy Agenda (PCL-R), characterized sociopathy as including an inner voice and feeling of good and bad, or ethical quality. Yet, that feeling of profound quality doesn't agree with social and normal practices. All things considered, individuals with sociopathy frequently legitimize activities they perceive as "wrong."

More or less, individuals with sociopathy may have little compassion and a propensity for defending their activities. However, they truly do realize the contrast among good and bad.

Psychopathy, as indicated by Bunny, includes no feeling of profound quality or sympathy.

Research from 2013 proposes the distinction among psychopathy and sociopathy may connect with contrasts in the cerebrum, including dim matter volume and amygdala improvement. For individuals with sociopathy, expanded neuron capability in specific pieces of the cerebrum might factor into the advancement of some feeling of profound quality.

What are the indications of sociopathy?
There's no standard rundown of sociopath signs, yet the signs and side effects of ASPD incorporate a steady example of dismissal for other people. For instance:

disregarding normal practices and regulations, or defying guidelines at the everyday schedule, violating social limits, taking, following and bugging others, and obliterating property
unscrupulousness and double dealing, including involving bogus characters and controlling others for individual addition
trouble controlling motivations and anticipating the future, or acting disregarding the results
forceful or bothered conduct, including regular battles or actual struggle with others
dismissal for individual security, or the wellbeing of others
trouble overseeing liabilities, including appearing at work, taking care of assignments, or covering rent and bills
practically zero responsibility or regret, or a propensity to legitimize activities that adversely influence others
Individuals with ASPD by and large show little inclination or interest in the existences of others. They may:

seem to be pompous or prevalent, with immovably fixed suppositions
use humor, knowledge, and charm to control
appear to be enchanting from the get go, until their personal responsibility turns out to be clear
Individuals with ASPD by and large find it trying to keep up with kinships, connections, and other commonly satisfying associations. This trouble might come from attributes, as:

low sympathy and the capacity to appreciate people on a deeper level
trouble gaining from botches
absence of worry for the wellbeing of others
a propensity to scare and undermine to keep up with control

What causes sociopathy?
Numerous specialists consider sociopathy a greater amount of an ecological develop than a hereditary one.

Indeed, mind science and acquired qualities have an influence, yet nurturing styles and childhood, alongside other ecological elements, convey the most weight. (Psychopathy, then again, seems connected to additional inborn organic elements.)

Youngsters who don't get supporting consideration from guardians will quite often grow up learning they need to deal with themselves, in light of the fact that no other person will. A few kids who experience misuse, brutality, and control since the beginning might come to display this way of behaving as they explore their own contentions.

Research additionally proposes it's feasible to "secure" sociopathy. Injury or harm to the cerebrums of the mind, which can occur because of a head injury or moderate circumstances, similar to dementia, can prompt a few reserved ways of behaving.

How could somebody be determined to have sociopathy?
Once more, remember that the DSM-5 sees no difference amongst sociopathy and psychopathy, or any different subtypes of ASPD.

Emotional wellness experts use DSM-laid out measures to analyze ASPD. This analysis can apply to somebody whose conduct lines up with the acknowledged meaning of either sociopathy or psychopathy.

A determination of ASPD expects no less than three of the seven signs recorded above, in addition to a couple of extra measures:

These ways of behaving show up across different everyday issues.
The individual is something like 18 years of age.
They had a few side effects of direct issue before the age of 15. This recognizes ASPD from lawbreaking conduct that starts in adulthood.

Withdrawn attributes and ways of behaving don't connect with schizophrenia or bipolar problem.
To make a finding, a specialist or therapist may:

pose inquiries about an individual's sentiments, contemplations, conduct, and individual connections
ask (with consent) relatives and better halves about their ways of behaving
assess their clinical history for indications of different circumstances
Remember that behavioral conditions, including APSD, include qualities that are outside of the individual's reach. These qualities go past a longing for individual increase and will quite often stay fixed over the long haul, causing trouble.

Might it at some point be an alternate condition?
Other psychological wellness conditions can include side effects like ASPD:

Discontinuous unstable problem (IED) includes outrageous and rehashed verbal or actual eruptions. These explosions, driven by motivation or outrage, can be coordinated toward individuals, property, or creatures. IED generally starts in youthfulness and normally before the age of 40. All alone, it doesn't include low compassion or absence of regret.
Direct confusion includes reserved conduct that normally starts by the age of 16. Specialists consider this condition a significant gamble factor for ASPD. Grown-ups should give indications of lead issue in youth

to be determined to have ASPD. Somebody who doesn't meet full ASPD standards may be determined to have lead jumble.
Schizophrenia frequently includes inconvenience perceiving facial feelings, a characteristic likewise association.

depression
trouble adapting to weariness or stress
substance use issues
Yet, since many individuals living with ASPD never decide to go to treatment, little examination on supportive treatment approaches exists. That doesn't mean treatment can't help. However, treatment and different methodologies by and large possibly work when somebody enthusiastically invests the energy.

Potential medicines for ASPD incorporate the accompanying.

Psychotherapy
Treatment includes conversing with a specialist about contemplations and sentiments that can provoke destructive or forceful way of behaving. It could likewise incorporate annoyance the board strategies or treatment for substance use.

Possibly helpful methodologies include:

Mental conduct treatment (CBT). CBT can assist individuals with figuring out how to consider their reactions to individuals and circumstances, which might prompt more useful ways of behaving. Treatment can, for instance, assist somebody with perceiving the advantages of utilizing exchange as opposed to savagery to address struggle or conflicts. CBT additionally includes psychoeducation, which can show individuals more ASPD.

Mentalization-based treatment (MBT). This approach plans to assist individuals with figuring out how to more readily recognize and grasp mental and profound attitudes — both their own and those of others. A little 2016 studyTrusted Source proposes MBT decreased antagonism and outrage, distrustfulness, self-hurt and relational hardships in individuals living with both ASPD and marginal behavioral condition, alongside prompting a better state of mind generally.

Popularity based helpful networks. This methodology, frequently utilized in penitentiaries, includes treatment gatherings of different sizes that assist members with pursuing cooperative choices as a component of a gathering and figure out together on issues influencing the local area. It can assist with supporting local area disapproved and prosocial thinking in individuals living with ASPD.

Possibility the board. This approach offers awards to empower treatment progress. More seasoned researchTrusted Source recommends it can assist with peopling living with ASPD limit admission of liquor and different substances.

Prescription

The Food and Medication Organization (FDA) hasn't supported any prescriptions to treat side effects of ASPD.

A specialist or specialist might suggest drug for side effects related with the condition, for example,

antipsychotics, as risperidone (Risperdal), as a first-line treatment for hostility
SSRI antidepressants, similar to fluoxetine (Prozac), or state of mind stabilizers, similar to lithium, to assist with treating hostility
anticonvulsants, as carbamazepine (Tegretol), to assist with lessening impulsivity
As per a little 2014 studyTrusted Source, the antipsychotic drug clozapine (Clozaril) shows some commitment as a treatment for men with ASPD. In the wake of taking the drug for a very long time, every one of the seven members experienced improvement in ASPD side effects, including outrage, impulsivity, and viciousness or hostility.

How would I adapt to somebody giving indications of sociopathy?
In the event that you might want to chip away at keeping up with your relationship with somebody who has ASPD, it might serve to:

remember they might in all likelihood never completely grasp your feelings

make sense of explicit ways their conduct influences others
lay out clear limits to safeguard your profound and actual space
urge them to get proficient help
Marriage or family mentoring can likewise assist you foster a more certain relationship with a friend or family member living with ASPD.

Eventually, they might decide not to regard your limits and keep on causing profound misery or actual damage. All things considered, cutting off the friendship, or if nothing else making space from it, might be your most secure choice.

Working with a specialist yourself can likewise help you:

investigate useful correspondence
assemble adapting abilities
distinguish indications of misuse
work on an arrangement to leave securely

PSYCHOPATHS

maniac is an individual having an egocentric and withdrawn character set apart by an absence of regret for one's activities, a shortfall of sympathy for other people, and frequently criminal tendencies."1

Numerous psychopathy qualities cross-over with side effects of total disregard for other people, a more extensive emotional well-being condition used to depict individuals who persistently carry on and disrupt guidelines. Be that as it may, just few people with total disregard for other people are viewed as a psychopath.2

Learn maniac qualities, the historical backdrop of the term, and how to perceive on the off chance that somebody may be a mental case. We likewise cover the distinctions between sociopath versus maniac, accessible medicines, and things you can do to adapt to this sort of individual.

Normal Mental case Qualities

Psychopathic conduct differs incredibly starting with one individual then onto the next. Some are sex guilty parties and killers, while others might find success pioneers. Everything relies upon their attributes. Recognizing a mental case and somebody with psychopathic traits is likewise significant.

It's feasible to display psychopathic qualities without being a real psychopath.3 Individuals with psychopathic attributes don't be guaranteed to participate in psychopathic way of behaving. Just people with psychopathic qualities who additionally display reserved conduct are viewed as sociopaths.

Psychopathic qualities generally include:4

Withdrawn conduct
Self-centeredness
Shallow appeal
Impulsivity
Insensitive, apathetic qualities
Absence of culpability
Absence of compassion
One investigation discovered that around 29% of everybody display at least one psychopathic qualities, however simply 0.6% are probably going to fit the meaning of a psychopath.5

Mental case versus Egomaniac
A few specialists accept that self-absorption and psychopathy exist on the very character continuum and that the two egomaniacs and mental cases will generally have low modesty and pleasantness, yet just an insane person likewise has low conscientiousness.6

Is There a Sociopath Test?
While there might be a lot of free "sociopath tests" drifting around on the web, two that are utilized most frequently are the Psychopathy Agenda Overhauled (PCL-R) and the Psychopathic Character Stock (PPL).

Psychopathy Agenda Updated (PCL-R): The PCL-R is a 20-thing stock that evaluates whether a singular displays specific qualities and ways of behaving that could show psychopathy. It's planned to be finished with a semi-organized interview and a survey of accessible records, for example, police reports or clinical data. This mental case test is frequently used to foresee the probability that a lawbreaker may re-insult, as well as their ability for restoration.

Psychopathic Character Stock (PPL): The PPL is an elective maniac test that was presented in 1996. This test is utilized to survey psychopathic characteristics in non-criminal populaces. It might in any case be utilized with detained people, however is all the more frequently applied to different populaces, like college understudies.

Indications of a Mental case

Psychopathic characteristics might arise during youth and deteriorate with age.7 coming up next are probably the most well-known indications of a mental case.

Shallow Appeal

Mental cases are many times amiable on a superficial level. They're typically great conversationalists and offer stories that do right by them. Maniacs might be interesting and magnetic too.

Need for Feeling

A mental case loves energy. They like to have consistent activity in their lives, and they as often as possible need to live in the "fast track."

Regularly, a maniac's requirement for excitement includes defying guidelines. They might partake in the excitement of pulling off something, or they could try and like the way that they would be able "get found out" all of a sudden. Therefore, mental cases frequently battle to remain participated in dull or dreary undertakings, and they might be narrow minded of schedules.

Neurotic Lying

Maniacs lie to look great and escape inconvenience. They additionally lie to conceal their past untruths. In this way, they experience issues keeping their accounts straight once in a while as they fail to remember what they've said. Whenever tested by anybody, a maniac will just change their story in the future or improve current realities to fit the circumstance.

Gaudy Identity Worth

A maniac has a swelled perspective on themselves. They see themselves as significant and entitled. Insane people frequently feel legitimized to live as indicated by their own guidelines, and they believe that the regulations don't make a difference to them.

Manipulative

Mental cases are great at getting others to do what they need. They might play on an individual's responsibility while deceiving get another person to take care of their responsibilities for them.

Absence of Regret

A sociopath doesn't mind at all what their conduct means for others. They might disregard something that harms somebody, or they might demand that others are blowing up when their sentiments are harmed. At last, sociopaths don't encounter culpability for causing individuals torment. They frequently excuse their way of behaving and fault others, truth be told.

Shallow Effect

Insane people don't show numerous feelings — basically not certifiable ones. They might seem cold and dispassionate a large part of the time. Be that as it may, when it serves them well, a mental case could show a sensational presentation of sentiments. These are typically brief and very shallow.

For instance, a maniac might show outrage on the off chance that they can scare somebody, or they could show misery to control somebody. However, they don't actually encounter these feelings.

Absence of Sympathy

Mental cases battle to comprehend how another person could feel apprehensive, miserable, or restless. It simply doesn't sound good to them as they're not ready to understand individuals. An insane person is totally unconcerned with individuals who are enduring — in any event, when it's a dear companion or relative.

Parasitic Way of life

Sociopaths might have tragic accounts about why they can't bring in cash, or they could frequently report being misled by others. Then, at that point, they exploit the generosity of others by relying upon them monetarily. A mental case utilizes individuals to get anything they can without really considering how the other individual might feel.

Poor Social Controls

Sociopaths battle to adhere to guidelines, regulations, and approaches a large part of the time. Regardless of whether they set off on a mission to observe the guidelines, an insane person generally doesn't adhere to them for a really long time.

Absence of Sensible, Long haul Objectives

A mental case's objective may be to become rich or popular. In any case, regularly, they have little thought regarding how to get these things going. All things considered, they demand that in some way, they'll get what they need without investing the energy to arrive.

Impulsivity

Maniacs answer things as indicated by the manner in which they feel. They don't invest energy contemplating the possible dangers and advantages of their decisions. All things considered, a maniac needs quick satisfaction. In this way, they might leave a place of employment, cut off a friendship, move to another city, or purchase another vehicle spontaneously.

Recklessness

Guarantees make next to no difference to a maniac. Whether they vow to reimburse a credit or sign an agreement, they aren't reliable. They might disregard kid support installments, get profoundly in the red, or disregard commitments and responsibilities.

A sociopath doesn't acknowledge liability regarding the issues in their lives. They see their issues as continuously being another person's shortcoming. Mental cases much of the time assume the part of the person in question and appreciate sharing tales about how others enjoy taken benefit of them.

Numerous Conjugal Connections

Mental cases might get hitched in light of the fact that it serves them well. For instance, they might need to spend an accomplice's pay or offer their obligation with another person. In any case, their way of behaving frequently prompts continuous separations as a sociopath's accomplice will ultimately see them in a more precise light.

Criminal Flexibility

Mental cases will generally see rules as ideas — and they typically consider regulations to be limitations that keep them down. Their criminal ways of behaving can be very shifted. Driving infractions, monetary infringement, and demonstrations of viciousness are only a couple of instances of the variety of wrongdoings an insane person could carry out.

Obviously, not all mental cases become detained. Some might work under obscure organizations or take part in untrustworthy practices that don't prompt a capture.

Disavowal of Restrictive Delivery

Most mental cases don't comply with the guidelines of contingent delivery when they are set free from jail. They might figure they will not get captured in the future, or they track down ways of pardoning their way of behaving. A maniac could try and fault "getting found out" on others.

Maniac Side effects or Signs

An individual who is manipulative, unscrupulous, self-centered, unremorseful, non-sympathetic, and shifty might be a sociopath. Culpability, indiscrimination, and absence of obligation are additionally normal attributes related with psychopathy.

Insane person versus Sociopath

While "insane person" and "sociopath" are now and again utilized interchangeably, they have various implications and various examples of attributes and ways of behaving. What's the distinction between maniac versus sociopath?

Maniacs miss the mark on soul and don't feel sympathy for other people. They might profess to mind, however frequently keep a typical exterior to conceal merciless or even criminal behaviors.8

Sociopaths might encounter restricted compassion and regret for their activities. They battle to keep up with ordinary ways of behaving and schedules and can be indiscreet and excessively profound. A sociopath might perceive that their activities are off-base yet track down ways of justifying their hasty and hurtful ways of behaving.

How Sociopaths Are Unique in relation to Maniacs

1:58

Get more familiar with the Distinction Among Mental cases and Sociopaths

This video has been therapeutically assessed by Rachel Goldman, PhD, FTOS.

Reasons for Psychopathy

Early exploration on psychopathy proposed that it frequently comes from issues connected with parent-kid connection. Close to home hardship, parental dismissal, and an absence of warmth were undeniably remembered to build the gamble that a kid would turn into a psychopath.9

Studies have tracked down a connection between abuse, misuse, uncertain connections, and successive partitions from parental figures. A few scientists accept that these youth issues can set off psychopathic traits.10

However, different specialists recommend it could be the reverse way around. Messes around with serious social issues might wind up with connection issues on account of their way of behaving — their wrongdoing could drive grown-ups away from them.11

Almost certainly, psychopathic attributes originate from a few variables, like hereditary qualities, neurological changes, unfriendly nurturing, and maternal pre-birth gambles, (for example, openness to poisons in utero).12

Insane people and Viciousness

Some writing proposes that a mental case might be bound to be brutal than everybody. Many examinations have connected psychopathic characteristics to savagery. Court frameworks might assess a lawbreaker's psychopathic inclinations as a method for foreseeing the probability that they will commit further brutal acts.13

Maniac Models

Notable sociopaths who participated in brutal criminal way of behaving incorporate Ted Bundy, Charles Manson, and Jack the Ripper.

However, not all sociopaths are brutal. Some are even viewed as great individuals. Studies have found there are "effective insane people" who are bound to be elevated to administrative roles and less inclined to spend time in jail in the slammer.

Effective maniacs might rank higher in specific qualities, like scrupulous characteristics, and this might assist them with dealing with their standoffish driving forces better compared to the people who end up sentenced for serious violations.

Treatment for Mental cases

Whether mental cases can be dealt with is a generally discussed issue. A few scientists report that treatment doesn't help. Others contend that particular medicines can lessen specific ways of behaving, like savagery.

A 2018 survey of the writing found that a considerable lot of the investigations led on treatment viability simply applied to explicit populaces, like sex wrongdoers. Thus, the medicines that work with that populace may not work for other psychopaths.14

Essentially, female mental cases might require an alternate methodology. As a rule, they will quite often be less vicious than men, so their treatment may be marginally unique.

A similar writing survey tracked down that mental social treatment (CBT) might be powerful at times. Yet, further examination is expected to distinguish which mental rebuilding systems work best and how to utilize them with explicit populaces.
Why everyone around them who are looking for methods for dealing with stress. All things considered, being around an insensitive, dispassionate individual is extreme.

Whether you think your companion, chief, or relative may be a maniac, their way of behaving can negatively affect your mental prosperity if you don't watch out.

In the event that being around a sociopath is causing you a decent measure of misery, get proficient assistance. An emotional well-being proficient can assist you with laying out sound limits and perceive when you're in danger of being controlled so you can deal with yourself.

Something From Verywell

A maniac frequently shows characteristics and ways of behaving that are chilly, manipulative, solitary, and egotistical. These propensities have been connected to youth encounters, including abuse, dismissal, and absence of parental warmth, be that as it may, the specific causes are not surely known.

Individuals with mental case qualities might have an expanded gamble for brutality and criminal way of behaving, yet not all sociopaths are vicious hoodlums. Medicines, for example, CBT might assist with decreasing specific psychopathic ways of behaving and characteristics.

CHAPTER 4

THE USE OF LAWS OF SELF DEFENSE

It's a generally acknowledged rule that an individual might safeguard themselves from hurt under fitting conditions, in any event, when that conduct would typically comprise a wrongdoing. In the US overall set of laws, each state permits a litigant to guarantee self-protection when blamed for a brutal wrongdoing, as does the central government.

The particular standards relating to self-preservation shift from one ward to another, be that as it may. This article offers clarifications of the wide ideas that make up self-preservation regulation in the US, however you ought to really take a look at the laws of your specific purview to grasp the particular necessities for a case of self-protection.

What Is Self-Protection?

Self-preservation is characterized as the option to forestall enduring power or viciousness using an adequate degree of neutralizing power or savagery. This definition is basic enough all over, yet it brings up many issues when applied to genuine circumstances.

For example, what is an adequate degree of power or savagery while protecting oneself? What goes past that level? Imagine a scenario in which the expected casualty incited the assault. Do casualties need to withdraw from the brutality if conceivable? What happens when casualties sensibly see a danger regardless of whether the danger really exist? What might be said about when the casualty's trepidation is abstractly authentic, yet entirely impartially absurd?

As may be obvious, self-protection regulation is more muddled than it initially shows up. To deal with the horde circumstances where self-preservation emerges, states have created rules to decide when self-protection is permitted and how much power a casualty can use to safeguard themselves. As referenced, the specific standards vary between states, yet the contemplations are to a great extent the equivalent.

Is the Danger Up and coming?
When in doubt, self-preservation possibly legitimizes the utilization of power when it is utilized because of a quick danger. The danger can be verbal, the same length as it places the planned casualty in a prompt apprehension about actual mischief. Hostile words without a going with danger of prompt actual damage, in any case, don't legitimize the utilization of power justifiably.

Also, the utilization of power with good reason by and large loses avocation once the danger has finished. For instance, on the off chance that an attacker attacks a casualty at the same time, closes the attack and shows that there could be at this point not any danger of brutality, then the danger of peril has finished. Any utilization of power by the casualty against the aggressor by then would be viewed as retaliatory and not self-preservation.

Was the Apprehension about Mischief Sensible?

Now and again self-preservation is legitimate regardless of whether the apparent attacker really mean the apparent casualty any mischief. What makes a difference in these circumstances is whether a "sensible individual" experiencing the same thing would have seen a prompt danger of actual damage. The idea of the "sensible individual" is a lawful vanity that is likely to contrasting translations by and by, however it is the general set of laws' best device to decide if an individual's impression of unavoidable peril legitimized the utilization of defensive power.

To show, picture two outsiders strolling past one another in a city park. Unbeknownst to one, there is a honey bee humming around his head. The other individual sees this and, attempting to be amicable, comes to rapidly towards the other to attempt to smack the honey bee away. The individual with the honey bee by his head sees a more peculiar's hand dart towards his face and fiercely stirs things up around town individual's hand away.

Defective Self-preservation

Some of the time an individual might have a veritable feeling of dread toward impending actual mischief that is unbiasedly preposterous. In the event that the individual purposes power to shield themselves from the apparent danger, the circumstance is known as "defective self-protection." Blemished self-preservation doesn't pardon an individual from the wrongdoing of utilizing viciousness, yet it can reduce the charges and punishments included. Only one out of every odd state perceives flawed self-protection, be that as it may.

For instance, an individual is sitting tight for a companion at a café. At the point when the companion shows up, he strolls toward the other individual with his hand waited for a handshake. The individual who had been standing by really fears that his companion means to go after him, despite the fact that this dread is absolutely preposterous. To stay away from the apparent danger, the individual hits his companion upside the head. While the individual's case of self-protection won't get him out of any lawbreaker accusations on account of the absurd idea of his insight, it could lessen the seriousness of the charges or the possible discipline.

A few states likewise consider examples where the individual guaranteeing self-preservation incited the assault as defective self-protection. For instance, on the off chance that an individual makes a contention that becomes vicious, unexpectedly kills the other party while protecting himself, a case of self-preservation could decrease the charges or discipline, yet wouldn't pardon the killing completely.

Relative Reaction

Self-protection regulation requires the reaction to match the level of the danger being referred to. All in all, an individual can utilize as much power as expected to eliminate the danger. Assuming the danger implies lethal force, the individual safeguarding themselves can show no mercy to neutralize the danger. In the event that, notwithstanding, the danger implies just minor power and the individual guaranteeing self-protection utilizes force that could inflict any kind of damage or demise, the case of self-preservation will fall flat.

Obligation to Withdraw

The first regulations with respect to self-preservation required individuals asserting self-protection to initially make an endeavor to stay away from the viciousness prior to utilizing force. This is otherwise called a "obligation to withdraw." While most states have taken out this standard for examples including the utilization of non-deadly power, many states actually expect that an individual make an endeavor to get away from the circumstance prior to applying deadly power.

Hold fast

Rather than the obligation to withdraw, many states have sanctioned supposed "hold fast" regulations. These regulations eliminate the obligation to withdraw and consider a case of self-preservation regardless of whether the petitioner nothing to escape from the danger of brutality. As referenced over, this is the more normal rule when circumstances include non-deadly power. State self-preservation regulations are parted on the hold fast standard when deadly power is in play, nonetheless.

Palace Regulation

Indeed, even in states that require an individual to withdraw from the danger of unavoidable damage prior to protecting themselves, an individual can frequently show no mercy against somebody who unlawfully enters their home. This standard, otherwise called "the palace principle," permits individuals to safeguard their homes against gatecrasher through deadly power. Like the vast majority of these principles, the specific outcomes.

CHAPTER 5

ROUTINE BULLYING PROOF HACKS THAT WORKS

Menaces ordinarily single out individuals that they believe are more vulnerable than they are, so face them. You may be terrified however on the off chance that you continue to confront them they'll stop.

Alternate ways of vanquishing your harasser and lose them track:
By boisterously saying "let me be"
Offer something amusing
Look at them without flinching and be pleasant to them
Keep out of the harasser's way
In the event that you fear your harasser stay away from where your domineering jerk hangs out, or take an alternate course to school. On the off chance that the domineering jerk doesn't see you, they can't menace you.

Utilize The Pal Framework Against Menaces
Menaces feel engaged to menace one individual, however seldom will they menace a gathering. Spend time with your companions. Assuming the domineering jerk wants to overcome the gathering, leave.

On the off chance that in the wake of utilizing these strategies and the harassing doesn't stop, it could be an ideal opportunity to request help. Make sure to tell somebody that you are being harassed. There are individuals who care about you and will help you.

Find support - Enlighten A Grown-up Regarding the Domineering jerk
It might appear to be frightening to tell somebody be that as it may, telling won't just get you help, it will cause you to feel less apprehensive. On the off chance that you are overall genuinely tormented and are in peril you should talk with a confided in grown-up right away. What's more, on the off chance that you can't go to your folks, search out a confided in educator life coach or school clinician.

In the event that you've told an adult previously and they haven't made any really meaningful difference with it, tell another person. Tell them precisely what occurred, who did the harassing, where and when it worked out, how long it's been going on to you, and how it's making you feel.When you tell your educator, life mentor or school clinician, ask them how they will assist with halting the harassing. They must assist with guarding you. Most grown-ups truly care about harassing and will give their very best for help you. Continue to tell until somebody helps you!

In the event that you are being tormented on the web ...

NEVER Answer
This could really exacerbate the harassing. Quickly tell your folks or a confided in relative. Have your folks block all interchanges from this individual. Make certain to save proof of cyberbullying. On the off chance that you receive a terrible email, print it out or save it so you can show it to a grown-up.

you ought to never answer cyberbullying . counting cyberbullying by text, email or texting. Do, be that as it may, save the messages, messages or texts for confirmation in the event that you really want it. It's perfect on the off chance that you can be valiant and bold and show the harasser you simply couldn't care less.

How NOT To Respond On the off chance that You Are Harassed

Don't...

Believe it's your issue. No one should be tormented!
Retaliate or menace an individual back
Remain quiet about it and simply trust the harassing will "disappear." Ensure you report the tormenting.

Play hooky or keep away from school or afterschool exercises since you're apprehensive about the domineering jerk

Be hesitant about the possibility of telling. Telling isn't squealing! It's the correct thing to do!

Hurt yourself. The fact that it can't be settled makes nothing that miserable. However agonizing as harassing may be, NOTHING is ever that terrible that you ought to hurt yourself in any capacity.

www.ingramcontent.com/pod-product-compliance
Lightning Source LLC
LaVergne TN
LVHW050348160826
845677LV00014B/3853

9798364516336